AlphaBasiCs

MEXICO

from A to Z

Bobbie Kalman & Jane Lewis

Crabtree Publishing Company

AlphaBasiCs

Created by Bobbie Kalman

To Sam Turton,
my favorite cosmic coincidence

Editor-in-Chief
Bobbie Kalman

Writing team
Bobbie Kalman
Jane Lewis

Managing editor
Lynda Hale

Editing team
Heather Levigne
Hannelore Sotzek
April Fast
Niki Walker

Computer design
Lynda Hale
John Crossingham

Production coordinator
Hannelore Sotzek

Separations and film
Dot 'n Line Image Inc.

Printer
Worzalla Publishing Company

Photographs
Jürgen Bavoni: pages 8 (all), 14 (middle), 27 (bottom left)
Jim Bryant: pages 13 (bottom), 19 (top), 22 (top right), 29 (top left)
Peter Crabtree: pages 14 (bottom), 22 (bottom right), 27 (bottom right),
   28 (bottom left)
Bobbie Kalman: pages 10 (bottom), 11 (all), 22 (bottom left), 26 (all)
James Kamstra: pages 12 (bottom), 13 (top both), 22 (top left),
   29 (bottom right)
Reuters/Bob Strong/Archive Photos: page 9
Jean Robertson: pages 14 (top), 27 (top)
Tom Stack & Associates: Byron Augustin: pages 6 (bottom),
   15 (bottom), 24 (top); John Cancalosi: pages 17 (bottom right),
   28 (bottom right); Chip and Jill Isenhart: page 23; Brian Parker:
   page 24 (bottom)
Magdalena Titian: pages 7 (top), 10 (top), 15 (top),
   17 (top both, bottom left), 19 (bottom), 28 (top both)
Other images by Digital Stock

Illustrations
Barbara Bedell: pages 16 (all except mug), 25
Antoinette "Cookie" Bortolon: pages 3, 10, 16 (mug),
   31 (calendar), back cover
Tammy Everts: page 31 (hieroglyphics)
Bonna Rouse: pages 4, 12-13, 18, 20, 23

Crabtree Publishing Company

350 Fifth Avenue
Suite 3308
New York
N.Y. 10118

360 York Road, RR 4
Niagara-on-the-Lake
Ontario, Canada
L0S 1J0

73 Lime Walk
Headington
Oxford OX3 7AD
United Kingdom

Cataloging in Publication Data

Kalman, Bobbie
   Mexico from A to Z

(AlphaBasiCs)
Includes index.

ISBN 0-86505-382-0 (library bound) ISBN 0-86505-412-6 (pbk.)
This book is an alphabetical introduction to the history, geography,
politics, culture, education, industries, and recreations of Mexico.

1. Mexico—Juvenile literature. 2. English language—Alphabet—
Juvenile literature. [1. Mexico. 2. Alphabet.] I. Lewis, Jane. II. Title.
III. Series: Kalman, Bobbie. AlphaBasiCs.

F1208.5.K34 1999   j972   LC 99-10548
                                                      CIP

Contents

All about Mexico	4
Beautiful beaches	5
Cities	6
Day of the Dead	8
Earthquakes	9
Fiesta	10
Geography	12
Homes	14
Industry	15
Jalapeños	16
Kids	17
Legend	18
Market	19
New Spain	20
Oceans	21
People	22
Quetzalcoatl	23
Religion	24
Spanish	25
Tourism	26
University	27
Village	28
Wildlife	29
Xiuhtecuhtli, Xipe Totec, and Xochiquetzal	30
Yucatán Peninsula	30
Zapotecs	31
Words to know & Index	32

A is **all about Mexico**! Mexico is a country in North America. It is south of the United States. California, Arizona, New Mexico, and Texas are the four states that share a border with Mexico. Mexico has two southern neighbors—Guatemala and Belize.

Quick facts about Mexico

Official name
United Mexican States
(Estados Unidos Mexicanos)

Population
97,563,400

Flag
(see page 18)

¡Hola!

Highest point
Mount Orizaba (5700 meters
or 18,700 feet above sea level)

Official language
Spanish

Government
Federal republic

Capital
Mexico City

Money
New Peso
(one Peso = 100 centavos)

Main religion
Roman Catholic

B is for **beautiful beaches**. White, sandy beaches can be found along Mexico's long coastlines. The warm waters of the Pacific Ocean, Gulf of Mexico, and Gulf of California surround the land of Mexico. Tourists visit **resorts** in Cancún (shown below), Acapulco, and Puerto Vallarta to enjoy the sun, surf, and sand for which Mexico is famous.

is for **cities**. Millions of people live in Mexico's cities and towns. The five largest cities are Mexico City, Guadalajara, Monterrey, Puebla, and Ciudad Juárez. Large cities in Mexico are similar to other North American cities. They have tall, modern buildings, subways, and parks. In many Mexican cities, traditional buildings stand alongside modern ones.

More than 20 million people live in Mexico City, shown left and below. It is one of the largest cities in the world and one of the oldest in North America. The Spanish built Mexico City in 1521 on the site of an ancient Aztec city.

(right) The buildings in the quiet, scenic town of San Miguel de Allende were built long ago by people who came from Spain. Today, it is against the law to tear down an old building or construct a new one in the town. Visitors to San Miguel can experience what a Mexican town looked like many years ago.

*(below) The town of Taxco is famous for its silver products. **Silversmiths** make jewelry and other items by hand. Some craftspeople work on the street. Tourists can watch them and purchase souvenirs on the spot.*

is for **Day of the Dead**. The Day of the Dead is a religious holiday celebrated on November 2. It follows All Saints' Day, which is celebrated on November 1. Many Mexicans believe that the spirits of their dead relatives return to visit them on these days. People welcome the spirits with food, parades, fireworks, parties, and skeleton decorations!

*On the first two days of November, families visit the cemetery to decorate the graves of their **ancestors** with food, flowers, and candles.*

E is for **earthquakes**. An earthquake is a trembling movement in Earth's **crust**, or surface. The crust is made up of several **plates**, or pieces, of rock. These plates shift slowly. Sometimes the plates push against one another, causing the ground to shake. Mexico is located in an **earthquake zone**, which is an area where many earthquakes occur.

Most earthquakes are small, but some are large enough to cause serious damage. In 1985, a terrible earthquake shook Mexico City. Thousands of people died when hundreds of buildings collapsed. Buildings in Mexico are now designed to withstand earthquakes.

F is for **fiesta**. Fiesta means "feast day" in Spanish, but the word is used to describe all kinds of parties and celebrations. Mexicans have many fiestas each year. Family and friends gather to enjoy music, dancing, food, games, and fireworks.

piñata

(above) No Mexican party would be complete without music! Musicians are often hired to play at fiestas.

(below) A **piñata** is part of many fiestas. Piñatas are colorful, papier-mâché containers filled with candy and small toys. They come in many shapes and sizes. Children take turns trying to break the piñata with a stick. When it breaks, the goodies inside spill out for everyone to share.

Mexicans hold **posadas**, or parades, during the nine nights before Christmas. Posada performers act out the Bible story of Mary and Joseph's journey to Bethlehem. They travel through the streets until they arrive at a house or hotel, which represents the inn where Jesus was born. One of the performers knocks on the door and asks if there is room for Mary and Joseph to spend the night. The posada actors and the "innkeepers" sing songs about whether Mary and Joseph can stay. Finally, the innkeepers tell them that they can sleep in the stable. Then everyone goes inside for a fiesta. At the posada shown below, goats, sheep, donkeys, and other animals made the "stable" seem realistic.

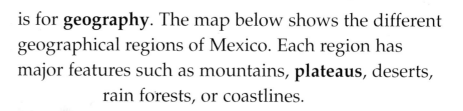

G is for **geography**. The map below shows the different geographical regions of Mexico. Each region has major features such as mountains, **plateaus**, deserts, rain forests, or coastlines.

The northwestern area of Mexico is a **desert** region. Few people live in this hot, dry area.

Baja California is a **peninsula**—an area of land with water on three sides. The Baja Peninsula is one of the longest in the world!

Mexico's east and west coasts are **lowlands**. The land is almost at sea level. The lowlands have a **tropical** climate.

desert

CENTRAL PLATEAU

BAJA CALIFORNIA

SIERRA MADRE OCCIDENTAL

The **Central Plateau** lies between two mountain ranges— the Sierra Madre Occidental and the Sierra Madre Oriental. It is a dry region high above sea level.

Almost half of Mexico's population lives in the **Central Highlands**, a region that is ideal for farming. Corn, beans, and cotton are grown there.

Rain forests are found in southern Mexico. A rain forest is a dense forest that grows in tropical regions. Many types of trees and plants grow in rain forests. Thousands of animal species also live there.

SIERRA MADRE ORIENTAL

CENTRAL HIGHLANDS

YUCATÁN PENINSULA

rain forest

is for **homes**. Mexicans live in many types of homes. In the country, most people live on farms. Some farm houses are made of **adobe**, or dried clay. Others are made of wood. In the city, most people live in houses or apartment buildings. Some Mexican homes are connected, and several families share a **courtyard**.

(left) Many people live in low-rise apartment buildings without elevators.

(above) Some Mexican homes are large, modern, and comfortable.

(right) This person lives in a smaller country home.
To learn more about village life, turn to page 28.

is for **industry**. An industry is made up of businesses that produce certain types of goods or offer services to people. Mexico's largest industries are oil, natural gas, mining, and steel production. Thousands of Mexicans make a living by working in tourism. This industry includes hotel employees and taxi drivers. Many people also support themselves by fishing.

Free Trade

Mexico has a trade deal with Canada and the United States called the North American Free Trade Agreement (NAFTA). This agreement allows the countries to trade many goods and services with one another without paying extra **duties**, or taxes.

J is for **jalapeños**. A jalapeño is a type of pepper that Mexicans use in their cooking. Jalapeños make food spicy! Corn, beans, and rice are the main ingredients used in many Mexican dishes. Mexican food is popular all over the world. Have you tried some of the foods shown below?

Be careful when you eat a jalapeño—the seeds and veins are the hottest parts of the pepper!

*A **tortilla** is a flat, round bread that is made from corn or wheat flour. Tortillas are a basic part of many Mexican meals.*

Guacamole

is a dip made from avocados. It is usually eaten with corn chips or spread onto tortillas before they are rolled into tacos.

*Mexicans make hot chocolate using a wooden tool called a **molinillo**. The molinillo makes the drink light and bubbly.*

*A **taco** is a tortilla folded around a filling of meat, cheese, beans, or vegetables. An **enchilada** is a taco covered in sauce.*

K is for **kids**. One-third of Mexico's population is under the age of fourteen. Children in Mexico attend school, do chores, and play games, of course!

(right) Many kids have jobs so they can earn money for their family. (below) Others help by caring for younger siblings.

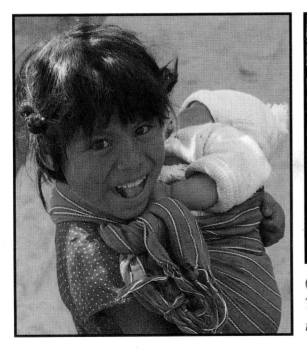

(above) Some children live far away from any city. This Mayan boy lives with his family in a village in the rain forests of southern Mexico.

is for **legend**. A legend is an old story of events people believe may be true. The eagle on the Mexican flag represents a legend about the capital of Mexico. In 1325, the Aztec people were searching for a place to build their capital city. One day, on an island in the middle of a lake, they saw an eagle perched on a cactus. It was eating a snake. The Aztecs believed this eagle was a sign from the gods telling them to build their city on that spot. The ancient city of Tenochtitlán, shown below, later became Mexico City.

M is for **market**. A market is a place where people buy goods such as clothing, food, handicrafts, and souvenirs. Most Mexican cities, towns, and villages have a marketplace. Some markets are set up inside a large building. Others are set up outside, where vendors sell their goods from stands in the street.

is for **New Spain**. In 1519, a Spanish explorer named Hernán Cortés sailed to the land that is now Mexico. Native Peoples, such as the Aztecs, had been living there for thousands of years. Cortés and his men fought against the Aztecs and took control of the land. The Spaniards called the land "New Spain" and ruled it for almost 300 years. By 1810, Mexicans no longer wanted Spanish rule, so they started a **revolution**. A revolution is a fight between people and their government. In 1821, the Mexican people won the revolution, and Mexico became an independent country.

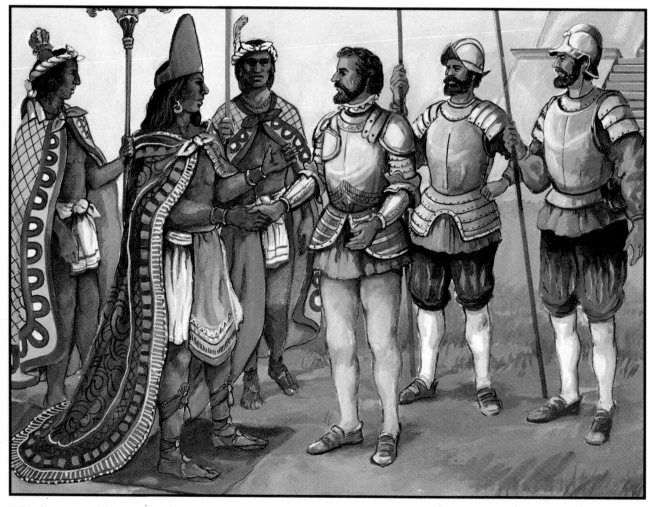

The first meetings between Cortés and the Native Mexicans were friendly. In the picture above, Cortés is greeting Montezuma II, the Aztec emperor. To learn how the Spanish explorer and his men defeated the Aztecs, turn to page 23.

is for **oceans**. There are several bodies of water around Mexico. The west coast of the country is edged by the Pacific Ocean. In the northwest, the Gulf of California lies between Baja California and Mexico's mainland. The Gulf of Mexico and the Caribbean Sea are found along the east coast.

*Many earthquakes occur in the Pacific Ocean off the coast of Mexico. These underwater quakes create huge waves called **tsunamis**. The waves travel at high speeds and hit Mexico's west coast with great force. Tsunamis damage trees and buildings along the shore.*

is for **people**. Who are the people of Mexico? A small part of the population is made up of Native Mexicans. They are the descendants of the peoples who lived in Mexico long ago. *Criollos* are people of European or Spanish descent. Not many people are entirely Native or Spanish, however. Most Mexicans are *mestizos*, or people of mixed Native and Spanish ancestry.

(below) The Maya, Huichol, Totonac, and Zapotecs are Native Mexicans.

(above) These three young Mexican boys are mestizos. They have both Native and Spanish ancestors.

(left and above) Many criollos are descendants of the Spanish people who came to Mexico in the 1500s. Others have moved there from Europe, Canada, and the U.S.A.

Q is for **Quetzalcoatl**. According to legend, Quetzalcoatl was a peaceful Aztec god who could change into a feathered serpent. Quetzalcoatl was a powerful god until Aztec priests forced him to "disappear." The priests wanted the Aztecs to worship more warlike gods. The people, however, believed that Quetzalcoatl would one day return to rule their land. When the Spanish explorer Cortés arrived in Mexico, he looked and talked unlike anyone the Aztecs had ever seen. The Aztecs thought that the powerful-looking Cortés was Quetzalcoatl, so they gave him control of their empire. When they realized that he was just a man, it was too late. Aztec warriors fought to win back their country from the Spaniards, but they lost the battle.

*The **quetzal** is a bird with long, beautiful feathers that lives in the rain forest. It was sacred to the Aztecs.*

Quetzalcoatl is pronounced ket-sal-KO-ah-tul. The name of the god comes from two words: quetzal is from the name of the bird, and *coatl* means snake.

23

R is for **religion**. Thousands of years ago, the Native Mexicans had their own religions. They worshiped many gods and goddesses. The Spaniards who took over Mexico in the mid-1500s were Roman Catholics. Roman Catholics are **Christians**. They wanted the Native Mexicans to give up their religions and accept Roman Catholicism instead. **Missionaries**, who were Catholic priests, were sent to **convert**, or change, the Native Mexicans to the Roman Catholic religion. The missionaries were successful, and today most Mexicans are Roman Catholics.

(left) Mexicans have many parades to celebrate Roman Catholic holy days, such as Easter.

(below) Mayans dressed in colorful outfits perform an ancient religious ceremony.

S is for **Spanish**. Before Hernán Cortés arrived in Mexico, there were many groups of Native Mexicans. Each group spoke a different language. After the Spaniards took over the country, however, they taught the Mexicans to speak Spanish. Today, Spanish is the national language of Mexico. Many English words have come from the Spanish language.

ahuacatl - avocado

la reata (the rope) - lariat

chilli - chili

cóyotl - coyote

xocolatl - chocolate

tomatl - tomato

sombrar (to shade) - sombrero

¿Hablas español?
(Do you speak Spanish?)

hola - hello

adiós - goodbye

gracias - thank you

buenos días - good morning

chico - boy

chica - girl

amigo - friend

bueno - good

is for **tourism**. Tourism is one of Mexico's major industries. It includes hotels, restaurants, shops, and taxis. Thousands of tourists come to Mexico every year because of the country's colorful culture, warm weather, and beautiful beaches. Tourism creates jobs for Mexicans. Money from tourism also pays for improvements such as new buildings and roads.

(right) Popular tourist areas such as Cancún, Acapulco and Puerto Vallarta are found along Mexico's coasts, where people can fish, swim, snorkel, and scuba-dive.

(bottom) The markets in towns and cities allow tourists to buy souvenirs at great prices!

is for **university**. Mexico is home to the oldest university in North America. The National University of Mexico was built in 1551 by the King of Spain, Charles V. In Mexico, children start their education with elementary school. They must attend school from age six to sixteen. They finish high school before they can enter university.

*The library at the National University of Mexico, shown left, is decorated with a **mosaic** of cultural scenes. A mosaic is a picture made up of many small pieces. The library's mosaic has almost seven million stone tiles!*

The pictures below show elementary and high-school students.

V is for **village**. Life in a small Mexican village is quieter than life in a big city. Some villages do not have electricity or running water. Most people who live in villages are farmers.

(above left) **Burros** *are used as a method of transportation in mountain villages. They can carry people and other heavy loads.*

(above right) This woman is carrying water home from the local well.

(above) The men in this community work together to lift a hydro pole. Soon there will be electricity in their village.

(left) Many villagers raise cattle. Spaniards brought the first cattle and horses to Mexico. Mexicans were the first cowboys of North America.

W is for **wildlife**. Wildlife are animals and plants that live naturally in the wild. There are many **species**, or types, of animals and plants in Mexico. Each region is home to different wildlife. Some animals live only in the hot, dry desert; others are in the hot, wet rain forest. Many animals and plants need the cooler air in the mountains and plateaus to survive.

Lizards (above), snakes, badgers, desert tortoises, scorpions, coyotes, and many types of cactuses can be found in the northern desert.

Deer, mountain lions (right), bears, coyotes, sheep, and wolves live in Mexico's mountain and plateau regions.

Dolphins (left), gray whales, shrimp, oysters, and many types of fish such as tuna, swordfish, and sardines live in the oceans around Mexico.

In the south, Mexico's jungles and rain forests are home to a great variety of wildlife, such as monkeys, armadillos, and lush tropical plants. Parrots (left), pelicans, flamingoes, snakes, tapirs (right), and big cats such as ocelots and jaguars are just a few of the animals that live there.

is for **Xiuhtecuhtli**, **Xipe Totec**, and **Xochiquetzal**, two ancient gods and a goddess. Xiuhtecuhtli was the Aztec god of fire. Xipe Totec was the Zapotec god of spring. Xochiquetzal was the Aztec goddess of beauty. Native Mexicans worshiped hundreds of different **deities**. You can read more about Mexico's ancient history under the letter Z.

Y is for the **Yucatán Peninsula**, the easternmost part of Mexico (see map on page 13). The Maya, one of the first groups of people to inhabit Mexico, lived in the Yucatán Peninsula. The Maya built many cities, temples, and **pyramids** there. People who visit the Yucatán Peninsula today can see ruins of these ancient buildings. Many are hidden under rain forests that have grown over the ruins.

is for **Zapotecs**. The Zapotecs were a group of people who lived in Mexico two thousand years ago. They were among the first peoples to live in Mexico. The Olmecs, Maya, Teotihuacán, Toltecs, and Aztecs were other **civilizations**, or groups, that once lived in Mexico. Each group lived during different time periods—from around 1000 **B.C.E.** until the 1500s, when the Spaniards arrived.

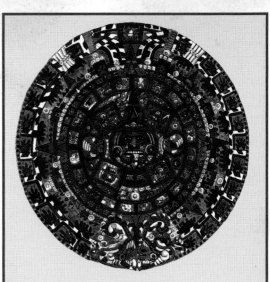

The ancient peoples of Mexico were skilled at mathematics, art, **astronomy**, **architecture**, and writing. If you are in Mexico, you can see how these ancient civilizations lived by visiting museums and the ruins of pyramids and temples. The Aztecs developed a calendar, which divided the year into 365 days. It showed important religious holidays as well as the movements of the Sun and Moon. The Aztec calendar, shown above, was painted in bright colors onto a huge, flat stone.

*These **hieroglyphics**, or pictures of words, were used by the Aztecs as a way of writing their language.*

The graph below shows the main time period of each civilization. Descendants of many of these groups live in Mexico today.

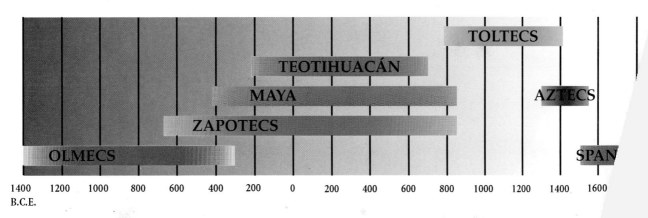

TOLTECS

TEOTIHUACÁN

MAYA

AZTECS

ZAPOTECS

OLMECS

SPAN

| 1400 | 1200 | 1000 | 800 | 600 | 400 | 200 | 0 | 200 | 400 | 600 | 800 | 1000 | 1200 | 1400 | 1600 |

B.C.E.

Words to know

ancestors The people from whom one is descended, such as grandparents and great-grandparents

architecture The design and construction of buildings

astronomy The study of the stars and planets

B.C.E. (Before the Common Era) Before the first year of the Christian calendar

burro A small donkey

Christian A person who follows the religious teachings of Jesus Christ

courtyard An outdoor area surrounded by walls

deity A goddess or god

federal republic Describing a country whose people elect a president

fiesta A Mexican celebration

missionary A person who travels to another country to teach religion

plateau A raised, flat area of land

pyramid A three- or four-sided structure that has a wide base and narrow top

resort An area to which people go for a holiday

revolution A war between people and their government

silversmith A person who works with silver

snorkel (verb) To swim under water while breathing through a tube

tropical Describing an area near the equator that is mainly warm and rainy

Index

ʼnimals 11, 13, 18, 23, 25, ʼ8, 29

ʼcs 6, 18, 20, 23, 30, 31

ʼs 5, 26

10, 17, 27

7, 9, 14, 17, 18, 30

ʼ, 21

28

1800 A.D.

5

31

ʼ1

history 18, 20, 23, 24, 30, 31

holidays 8, 11, 24, 31

homes 14, 28, 29

industry 15, 26

language 4, 25, 31

maps 4, 12-13, 21

markets 19, 26

Mayans 17, 22, 24, 30, 31

Mexico City 4, 6, 9, 18

Native Mexicans 6, 17, 18, 20, 22, 23, 24, 25, 30, 31

oceans 5, 21, 29

population 4, 13, 17, 22

pyramids 30, 31

rain forest 12, 13, 17, 23, 29, 30

religion 4, 8, 24, 31

school 17, 27

Spanish 4, 6, 7, 10, 20, 22, 23, 24, 25, 28, 31

tourism 5, 7, 15, 26, 30, 31

villages 14, 17, 19, 28

Yucatán Peninsula 13, 30

Zapotecs 22, 30, 31

1 2 3 4 5 6 7 8 9 0   Printed in the U.S.A.   8 7 6 5 4 3 2 1 0 9